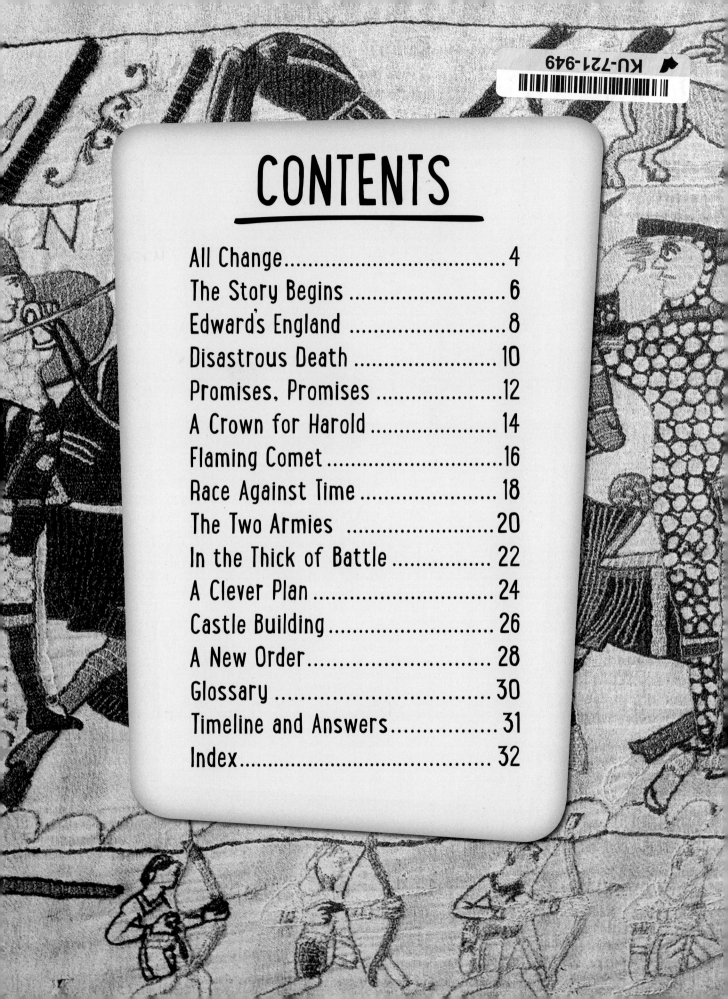

CONTENTS

ALL CHANGE

On 14 October 1066, there was a fierce battle near Hastings in southern England. The Battle of Hastings was between an English army, led by King Harold II, and an army from Normandy, in northern France. The battle helped decide the future of life in England.

The **Normans** were led by Duke William, who is often called William the **Conqueror**. The Normans (from 'North Men') were the **descendants** of **Vikings**. They spoke Norman French.

◄ A Norman lord might have fought with a mace (metal club), dagger, sword and shield.

HOW do we know?

In the 1070s, a giant **tapestry** was stitched to tell the story of the Battle of Hastings. Although it was made by English **craftswomen**, it is called the Bayeux Tapestry because it was kept at Bayeux in Normandy.

Go back to Normandy!

▲ The Bayeux Tapestry was probably made for Duke William's half-brother, Odo. It tells the story of the battle from the Norman point of view.

WHAT do you think?

How would you feel if your country was **invaded** by an army from another country?

THE STORY BEGINS

In 1002, King Aethelred II of England married Emma, the sister of Normandy's ruler. A year or so later, Emma had a son, called Edward. When Edward was 12 or 13, King Aethelred died. A Viking prince called Cnut seized the English throne.

▶ Edward is known as Edward the **Confessor** because he was very religious.

▶ This coin shows King Aethelred.

Vikings had been settling in England for 150 years. English and Viking lords often battled for the throne. Emma feared what Cnut might do to Edward, so she sent her son to Normandy. There Edward became friendly with the young Duke William (see page 4). By 1042, Cnut and his sons were dead, so Edward returned to England and was crowned king.

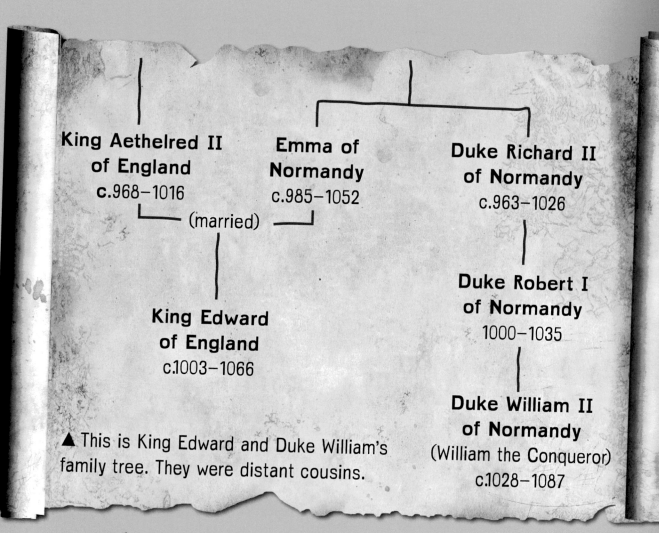

King Aethelred II of England
c.968–1016

Emma of Normandy
c.985–1052

Duke Richard II of Normandy
c.963–1026

(married)

King Edward of England
c.1003–1066

Duke Robert I of Normandy
1000–1035

Duke William II of Normandy
(William the Conqueror)
c.1028–1087

▲ This is King Edward and Duke William's family tree. They were distant cousins.

WHAT do you think?

Edward lived in Normandy for 26 years. Do you think he felt more 'English' or more 'Norman'? Why?

EDWARD'S ENGLAND

King Edward was an **Anglo-Saxon**. In the 5th century, thousands of Anglo-Saxons had started to arrive in England from Germany, the Netherlands and Denmark. The Anglo-Saxons ruled England, except when Vikings took control.

Most of the people who lived in Edward's kingdom were farmers or craftspeople. They were **Christians**. They obeyed their local lord, who usually obeyed the king. They spoke an old version of English. We can just recognise some of their words: 'cyning' meant king, and 'cild' meant child.

▼ Most Anglo-Saxons worked all day in the fields, growing crops and looking after animals.

Get to work, you lazy lot!

HOW do we know?

In 1161–3, a **monk** called Aelred of Rievaulx wrote a book about King Edward's life. Monks were among the few people who could read and write.

▲ This monk is writing with a quill (feather) dipped in ink. He holds a knife for scraping away mistakes.

▼ This is a **reconstruction** of an Anglo-Saxon village. Most buildings were wooden with thatched roofs.

FIND OUT FOR YOURSELF
What do these Anglo-Saxon words mean: 'aex', 'sweord' and 'scyld'?

DISASTROUS DEATH

On 5 January 1066, King Edward died after a short illness. He and his wife, Edith, did not have any children to **inherit** the throne. Three men claimed the English throne should be theirs. There was trouble ahead.

▶ Edward's body is placed in its **tomb** on 6 January 1066. He was buried in Westminster Abbey.

WHAT do you think?

To keep peace in his kingdom, what should King Edward have done before he died?

The first man was Harold Godwinson, Edith's brother. Harold claimed Edward promised him the throne as he lay dying. The second man was a Viking king, Harald Hardrada of Norway. He wanted to take back King Cnut's kingdom (see page 6). Harald Hardrada was supported by Harold Godwinson's brother Tostig, because the brothers had argued. The third man was Duke William of Normandy.

"I commend my wife and all my kingdom to your care."

King Edward's last words, according to Harold Godwinson

▲ In the first scene of the Bayeux Tapestry, King Edward is pointing at Harold Godwinson. Is Edward offering Harold his kingdom or giving him an order?

PROMISES, PROMISES

Duke William claimed his friend King Edward had promised he could inherit the English throne. William also claimed that Edward had sent Harold Godwinson to Normandy to confirm the promise. Harold told the story differently: he had stayed with William in Normandy but had made no promises.

Whatever the truth, William was keen to get his hands on England, because it had good farmland and rich towns.

William

Harold

▲ The Bayeux Tapestry tells William's version of the story. It shows Harold Godwinson promising to help William claim the English throne. Harold's hands are on **holy relics** as proof of his honesty.

HOW do we know?

In fact, we don't know anything for sure. All the written records we have are based on **word of mouth**.

WHAT do you think?

Who had the best claim to the English throne?

▲ During Harold's stay in Normandy, William entertained him at feasts like this one.

◀ William was born at the Castle of Falaise in Normandy. The castle was rebuilt after his death, as shown here.

A CROWN FOR HAROLD

When Edward died, Harold Godwinson was ready to act swiftly to take the throne. A group of English lords, called the **Witan**, met to decide who should be king. They agreed that Harold Godwinson had the best claim. Harold was crowned king the very next day.

The news soon reached Normandy. William decided to invade England and claim the throne for himself. He started gathering an army and building ships to cross the sea. Harald Hardrada and Tostig also laid plans to invade.

Congratulations, Your Majesty.

▶ Harold Godwinson took the throne on 6 January 1066.

<u>HOW</u> do we know?

A Norman priest called William of Poitiers wrote about Duke William's battle for England. He worked for William, which may be why he described the duke as a perfect hero.

FIND OUT FOR YOURSELF
In which building have all English kings and queens since Harold been crowned?

▼ The Bayeux Tapestry shows Norman workers cutting down trees and chopping them into planks to build ships for William.

FLAMING COMET

In April 1066, a burning light appeared in the sky over England. Today, we know the light was **Halley's Comet**, but then people feared it was a sign that something terrible was going to happen.

▶ In the Bayeux Tapestry, Halley's Comet is shown as a ball of flames.

What's that?

WHAT
do you think?

Why do you think people were worried by the comet?

Knowing William was about to invade, King Harold and his army waited on England's south coast. But in early September, the king heard that Harald Hardrada and Tostig had landed in northern England with a Viking army. King Harold rushed to the north. On 25 September, Harold defeated the Vikings at the Battle of Stamford Bridge. Over 10,000 Englishmen and Vikings were killed, including Harald Hardrada and Tostig.

> **"Harald Hardrada was hit by an arrow in the windpipe, and that was his death-wound."**
>
> Viking poet Snorri Sturluson

FIND OUT FOR YOURSELF
How often does Halley's Comet appear?

▼ Harald Hardrada sailed from Norway in ships like these.

RACE AGAINST TIME

On 28 September 1066, William landed at Pevensey Bay on England's south coast with an army of 8,000 men. To protect themselves, they built a wooden castle at nearby Hastings.

When the news of William's arrival reached Harold, he raced south with his remaining men. Many tired soldiers ran away, so Harold lost time rounding up more. On 13 October, Harold set up camp with about 8,000 men on Caldbec Hill, 12 kilometres from William's castle.

HOW do we know?

We can visit Hastings Castle, where the ruins of a stone castle stand on the site of William's wooden castle.

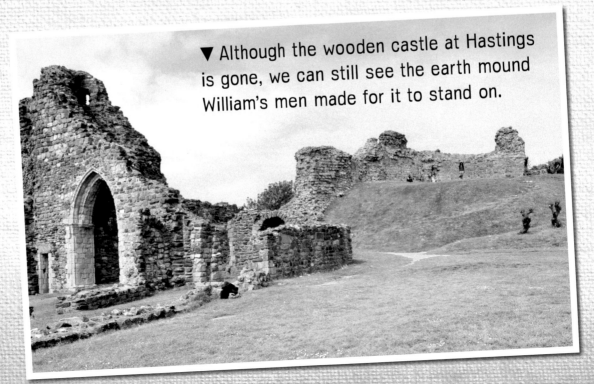

▼ Although the wooden castle at Hastings is gone, we can still see the earth mound William's men made for it to stand on.

▼ This map shows where the events of 1066 took place.

WHAT do you think?

King Harold camped on a hill. Why was this a good position?

▼ William's men build a **motte and bailey** ('mound' and 'fenced area') castle.

SCOTLAND

Harold's route - - - ~ ~
William's route - - - ~ -

IRELAND

Stamford Bridge ✗

ENGLAND

WALES

London ●

▼ War horses are unloaded from William's ships.

✗ 🏰 Hastings

⛵ Pevensey Bay

FRANCE

● Falaise

NORMANDY

19

THE TWO ARMIES

Harold had about 1,000 **trained** soldiers, called houscarls. They wore a helmet and **chainmail** tunic, and carried a shield and battle-axe. All his other men were untrained farmers. They had only a shield for protection, and fought with a farmer's tool, dagger or spear. Hardly anyone had a bow and arrow. Horses were so expensive that no Englishman would risk one on the battlefield.

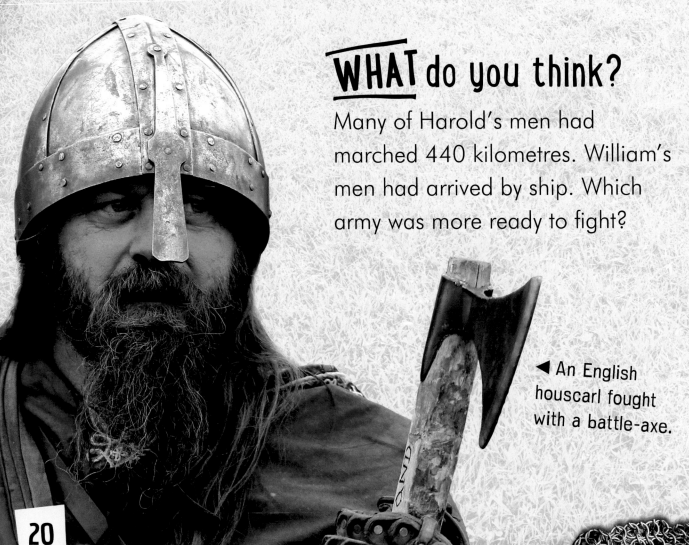

WHAT do you think?

Many of Harold's men had marched 440 kilometres. William's men had arrived by ship. Which army was more ready to fight?

◄ An English houscarl fought with a battle-axe.

William's army had better training and weapons. A quarter of his 8,000 men were armed with bows and arrows. Another quarter were skilled **knights** who rode into battle on horseback.

◄ Norman bows and arrows could kill the enemy from a distance.

HOW
do we know?

If we look closely at the Bayeux Tapestry, we can find out about fighting styles and weapons.

▲ Norman knights used the tactic of riding straight at the enemy while holding a **lance**.

IN THE THICK OF BATTLE

At dawn on 14 October, William marched his men toward the English army. The English stood shoulder to shoulder on the hill, forming a wall with their shields. At 9 a.m., the Normans fired their first arrows. The steep slope meant that the arrows could not pierce the wall of shields. William sent forward soldiers armed with spears, then his knights. But the English stayed firm.

▼ A Norman knight rides among his men in this **re-enactment** on the site of the battlefield.

FIND OUT FOR YOURSELF
Harold's brothers Gyrth and Leofwine fought at Hastings. What happened to them?

The story spread amongst the Normans that William had been killed. They started to **retreat**. Some English warriors chased them, but were surrounded and killed. William rode among his men to show he was alive.

▼ This re-enactment of the battle shows the English wall of shields.

" The English met missile with missile,
Sword-stroke with sword-stroke... "
Poem by the Norman bishop Guy of Amiens

A CLEVER PLAN

William thought about how the English soldiers were killed when they chased the Normans. He came up with a plan. He ordered his men to pretend to run away. Each time they did it, some of the English chased them — and were killed. The Normans began to break through the wall of shields.

Late in the afternoon, King Harold was killed. Some people said an arrow pierced his eye. Others said William stabbed him. When the English heard their king was dead, many fled. By dusk, the Normans had won.

▶ In this 13th-century illustration, William is stabbing Harold with his lance.

▼ This scene in the Bayeux Tapestry is labelled in Latin: 'Here King Harold has been killed'. But is he the man with the arrow in his eye or the one trampled under the horse? No one knows for sure.

Harold?

Or Harold?

HOW do we know?

Today we can visit Battle Abbey, which William built to remember the soldiers who died in the Battle of Hastings.

FIND OUT FOR YOURSELF
What materials were arrows made from?

▶ Battle Abbey stands near the site of the battle.

CASTLE BUILDING

Now William marched on England's largest city, London. After defeating bands of angry Londoners, William was crowned King William I of England in Westminster Abbey on 25 December 1066. But he still needed to control the rest of the country.

William ordered castles to be built up and down the country, and along the borders with Wales and Scotland. Safely based in these castles, William's lords defeated everyone who fought against them. At first, William's castles were wooden. Later, he built the first stone castles in England. Stone was harder to burn or knock down.

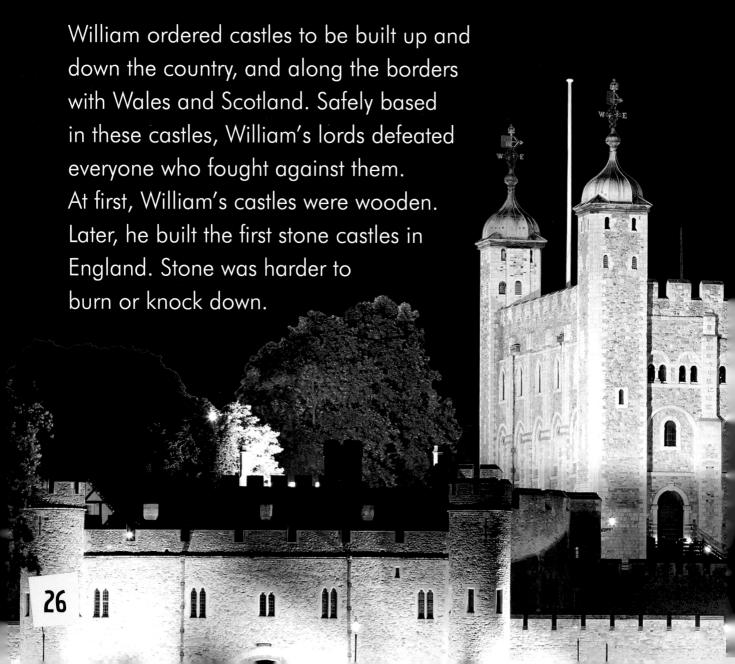

WHAT do you think?

The new stone castles towered over English homes. How do you think they made the English feel?

▼ The White Tower, part of the Tower of London, was the first stone castle William built in England.

sooo heavy!

▲ Workers build a castle, using a simple machine called a pulley to lift stones.

FIND OUT FOR YOURSELF
About how many castles were built in England while William was king?

A NEW ORDER

William and his sons and grandchildren ruled England until 1154. The Normans changed English life for ever. William took away almost all land from the English and gave it to Norman lords. In return, the Norman lords gave the king knights to fight for him. Ordinary people were allowed small plots of land, for which they paid their lord with money, crops or work.

At first, the English still spoke Anglo-Saxon, but thousands of Norman French words – such as 'colour', 'favourite' and 'marriage' – soon crept in. In time, everyone was speaking an English much closer to what we speak today.

◄ William gives English land to a Norman lord. In return, the lord and his knights promise their loyalty and help to the king.

FIND OUT FOR YOURSELF

What relation is Queen Elizabeth II to William the Conqueror?

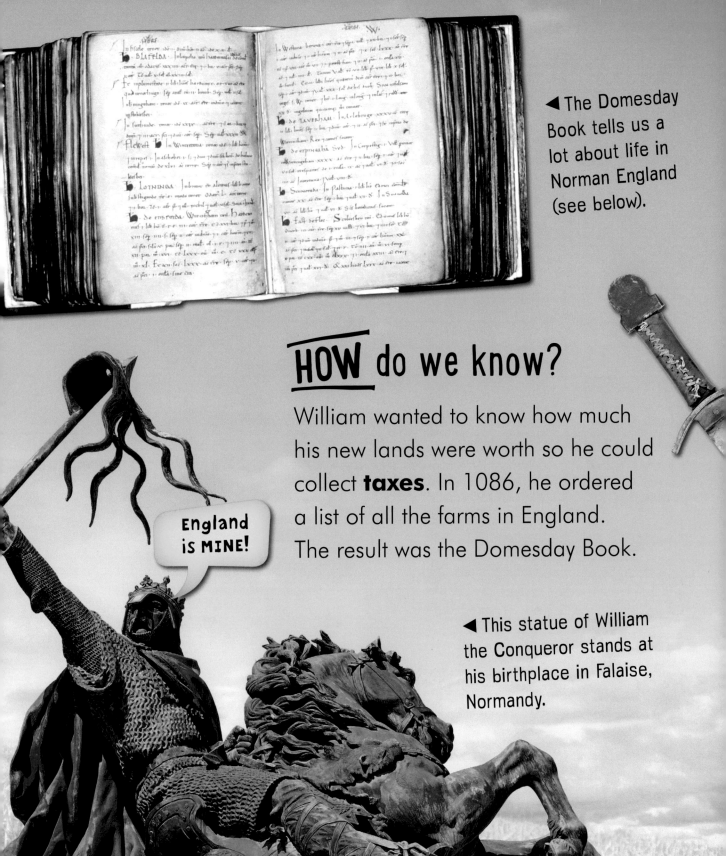

◀ The Domesday Book tells us a lot about life in Norman England (see below).

HOW do we know?

William wanted to know how much his new lands were worth so he could collect **taxes**. In 1086, he ordered a list of all the farms in England. The result was the Domesday Book.

England is MINE!

◀ This statue of William the Conqueror stands at his birthplace in Falaise, Normandy.

GLOSSARY

Anglo-Saxons – tribes such as the Angles, Saxons and Jutes, who ruled England from about 450 until 1066

c. – short for 'circa', which means 'about'; it is often used with dates

chainmail – armour made from metal rings linked together

Christian – follower of the religion based on the teachings of Jesus

confessor – a person who declares their faith in God

conqueror – a person who takes control of a place by using force

craftswomen – women who make goods, such as cloth or pots, by hand

descendants – people who are related to a group of people or person who lived in the past

Halley's Comet – a comet named after astronomer Edmond Halley; a comet is a mass of ice, gas and dust that travels round the Sun

holy relics – the belongings or body parts of a dead holy person

inherit – receive something of value from a person after their death

invaded – entered by an enemy army

knight – a horseriding warrior who fought for a lord in return for land

lance – a strong spear held by a knight

monk – a man who lives in a Christian group in a home called a monastery

motte and bailey – a simple castle with a tower on an earth mound, surrounded by a fence and ditch

Normans – a Viking people who settled in northern France in the 10th century

reconstruction – rebuilding a house or other building as it used to be

re-enactment – acting out an event

retreat – move away from the enemy

tapestry – a cloth with pictures stitched or woven into it

taxes – money paid to the government

tomb – a burial place for a dead person

trained – having been taught skills

Vikings – peoples from Norway, Sweden and Denmark who first raided, then settled across Europe from the 8th century

Witan – a group of lords who advised the Anglo-Saxon king or queen

word of mouth – information spoken from one person to another

TIMELINE

c.1022	Harold Godwinson is born in England.
c.1028	William the Conqueror is born in Normandy, France.
1042	Edward the Confessor becomes king of England.
5 Jan 1066	King Edward dies, leaving no children to take the throne.
6 Jan 1066	Harold Godwinson is crowned King Harold II of England.
14 Oct 1066	William the Conqueror defeats King Harold at the Battle of Hastings.
25 Dec 1066	William I is crowned the first Norman king of England.
1154	Norman rule ends when the Plantagenet family, led by William's great grandson Henry II, takes the throne.

FIND OUT FOR YOURSELF ANSWERS

p9 Axe, sword and shield.
p15 Westminster Abbey.
p17 Every 75–6 years.
p22 They died in the battle.
p25 Iron, wood and goose feathers.
p27 Around 500 – or even more.
p28 28th great-granddaughter.

INDEX